Sun, Sage & Sand

*A pictorial journey
through the
Okanagan, Similkameen,
Shuswap, Thompson and
the Nicola regions of
British Columbia*

William Bradley Jurome

Photographs and Text:
William Bradley Jurome

Colour processing:
One Hour Photo, Kelowna,
Pat Deleenheer, Chris Hill

Colour Seperations:
LithoTech Canada, Burnaby

Layout:
J.D. (Jack) Thompson

Lithography:
Ehmann Printing Ltd., Kelowna

Binding:
Northwest Book Co., Burnaby

originally published by:
the Okanagan Mainline Real Estate Board,
1969, 1972, 1975.

Canadian Cataloguing in Publication Data

Jurome, William Bradley, 1930 -
Sun, sage & sand; a pictorial journey
through the Okanagan, Similkameen,
Shuswap, Thompson and the Nicola regions
of British Columbia

Includes index.
ISBN 0-929041-00-3 (bound) -
ISBN 0-929041-01-1 (pbk.)

1. Okanagan-Similkameen (B.C.) --
Description and travel.   2. Shuswap Lake
Region (B.C.) -- Description and travel.
3. Thompson-Nicola (B.C.) -- Description
and travel.   I. Title.

FC3812.J87 1989   917.11'4'044
C89-090116-3   F1087.8.J87 1989

Published by: DACONA GRAPHICS INC.
P.O. Box 2069, Station "R"
Kelowna, B.C. V1X 4K5

Printed and bound in Canada

Contents

Foreword

*A*s you turn the pages of this book, you will be taken on a delightful pictorial journey through the beautiful valleys of the Okanagan, Similkameen, Shuswap, Nicola and the Thompson. This region of British Columbia is touched on the west by the towering Cascade Mountains and on the south by the Canada/U.S.A. border. The imposing Rogers Pass guards its northern gateway, while to the east rise the mighty Monashee Mountains.

The people of this region live and work in a land of unparalleled beauty and diversity. The river valleys cradle lush fruit orchards and vineyards, fields of sweet corn, vegetables, hay and grain. On the foothills, dotted with fragrant sage, herds of cattle browse contentedly on golden bunch grass. The hills are dark with lush forests, where tall stands of Spruce, Douglas Fir, and Ponderosa Pine still grow in virgin splendour. Fine roads and highways connect bustling towns and major cities, which are strategically located throughout the region, providing commercial and domestic services to a dynamic and enterprising population.

The entire region is a paradise for tourists and visiting sportsmen. Fish and game are plentiful. There are many lakes and rivers offering unparalleled boating, spectacular sailing, fishing, and other water sports. Campgrounds are scattered generously throughout the beautiful forests and parks. Clean, warm, sandy beaches beckon the summer fun seekers; while in winter, challenging ski runs and scenic snow covered meadows are close by to delight the hardy alpine and nordic skier. Championship golf courses abound, challenging the most skilled professional as well as the enthusiastic duffer. Famous resorts proudly offer luxurious accommodations and provide diverse activities for their many guests. A holiday here might include, a quiet walk in the woods or a vigorous hike or climb in the mountains. A group of friends, or a family, may enjoy a sailing cruise or an excursion on a houseboat, perhaps taking a week or more to explore the many miles of scenic shoreline. For the more adventurous, there are river rafting expeditions mountain biking or horse back riding and packing trips. There are back road safaris by all-terrain vehicle or snow mobile. Hunters may pursue their favorite big game in season.

For the fishermen, this region offers untold opportunities. Crystal clear streams give up gleaming Golden Brook Trout. Placid mountain lakes abound with Rainbow Trout. The larger lakes, Okanagan and Shuswap, produce bigger fish including the famous "Kamloops Trout". Many of these are taken each year in trophy sizes ranging to 25 pounds. The rivers of the Thompson and the lower Shuswap system produce each year a run of "Steelhead", the famous sea-going trout that is by all accounts the premier fighting fish of the north-west rivers. Many fishermen have long tried, but only a few have experienced the exhilaration of landing one of these fine fish.

To experience for yourself through the magic of colour photography, this land and its many diverse attractions, I invite you to join me now as we embark upon a pictorial journey through this majestic and fascinating land of "Sun, Sage & Sand".

William Bradley Jurome

PONDEROSA PINES, glow warmly in the late afternoon light. This group of stately trees guard a grassy glen along Highway 3 near the town of Princeton.

ALONG THE HOPE-PRINCETON Highway we can see the Similkameen River near its source high in the Cascade Mountains. Here, Cottonwoods in their fall cloak cast a warm glow over cool evening shadows, along Highway 3 near Allison Pass.

THE SIMILKAMEEN RIVER glides silently by groves of golden Poplars at sunset along Highway 3 near Princeton.

THE TOWN OF PRINCETON at the confluence of the Similkameen and Tulameen Rivers was once known as "Vermilion Forks" because of a deposit of vermilion ochre found nearby on the Tulameen River. Tulameen is the Indian name for "Red Earth". Indian tribes, in those days, came from afar to barter for the red earth which they used for body paint. Renamed "Princeton" in 1860 after the Prince of Wales, it became, an important mining, trading, and rail centre. Names such as "Coalmont", "Granite Creek", "Copper Mountain", and the "Kettle Valley Railway" bring back exciting memories of Princeton's legendary past. Copper Mountain has disappeared, replaced by a modern open-pit mining operation. Coalmont is now a ghost-town. The thundering rails of the Kettle Valley Railroad now lay silent. Today, in quieter times, this neat little town still welcomes the many visitors who travel the Hope-Princeton Highway.

THE PIKE MOUNTAIN RANCH GATE, as we can see, displays many fine trophies of the excellent big game hunting for which this area is justly famous.

ALLISON LAKE, shown here, is but one of many in a string of beautiful lakes that we find as we drive along scenic Highway 5 north of Princeton. There are hiking trails and a fine picnic site at the south end of this lake.

A HERD OF PONIES graze peacefully enjoying their leisure time. All too soon these working ranch horses will, no doubt, be busy with the coming roundup.

AN OLD LOG CABIN, its logs and shakes bleached and weathered by time and the elements, still stands. It reminds us of the sturdy pioneers that first settled and worked this land.

HIGHWAY NO. 5 between Princeton and Merrit winds through lush green valleys, past crystal lakes and scenic ranchlands.

OVERLEAF: we visit two of the beautiful lakes that are typical of this area. A gigantic derelict old pine lies on the shore of Courtenay Lake, while at a ranch near Aspen Grove, a group of horses wait in a barnyard corral to be saddled.

5

BROMLEY ROCK is a favourite stop for many who travel Highway No. 3. A fine picnic site and swimming hole make this a most popular choice for the family traveling this way in the summer.

OLD MINE AND MILL RUINS were the one feature that most recent travelers remember of the town of Hedley. Site of the fabulously rich "Mascot Mine" of old, the town today , after languishing for many years, again bustles with renewed mining activity.

THE SIMILKAMEEN RIVER VALLEY south of Hedley is bracketed by rugged mountains. Often, mountain goats can be seen roaming the craggy cliffs near the highway.

THE CHURCH OF ST. ANN'S stands on a dry ridge east of Hedley. This historic little church is located at the Indian Village of Chuchuawa.

THE OLD RED BRIDGE near Keremeos at one time carried the locomotives and trains of the Great Northern Railway. Today, this picturesque bridge is the gateway to the spectacular Ashnola River Valley and the Cathedral Lakes Provincial Park.

THE TOWN OF KEREMEOS lies in the heart of the beautiful Similkameen Valley. This tidy little town is often called "The Fruit Stand Capital of Canada" after the many road-side fruit stands that line the highway. Here, local fruit and vegetable growers proudly offer their produce for sale to the appreciative traveller. It seems that the growers are determined to out-do each other in their quest to lure customers off the highway with delightfully colourful and tempting displays of luscious fruits and vegetables. The combination of endless sunshine, rich valley bottom soil irrigated with the sweet water of the Similkameen, produces fruits and vegetables here that are of outstanding quality and flavour. Much of the crop is packed commercially and shipped, but a great quantity of the fruit is allowed to tree ripen each year; then it is sold at the colourful road-side stands. Indeed, many travelers from far and wide make a special pilgrimage here each summer to enjoy their favourite tree ripened fruit, plump, luscious and sweet.

The surrounding mountains and valleys of the Similkameen and Ashnola provide the visitor with a wondrous, incredibly scenic playground. Wildlife is plentiful. White-tailed deer, mountain sheep, and goats are often seen in the vicinity. Outdoorsmen come here in great numbers to enjoy the many hiking trails. Some of the more spectacular being in the "Cathedral Lakes Provincial Park", which caters to and is accessible to hikers and backpackers only.

Many years ago, this beautiful Similkameen Valley echoed to the sounds of the puffing locomotives and rumbling trains of the Great Northern Railway which moved supplies to and from the then busy mining towns of Princeton and Hedley. Today the rails and tracks are mostly gone. The old railbed, however, can be clearly seen in many places; a case in point being "The Old Red Bridge" located just west of Keremeos on the Ashnola River Road. This picturesque old bridge was originally built and used by the Great Northern as a railroad bridge.

AT CAWSTON, the Similkameen River flows through a broad valley lush with fruit orchards, vineyards and fields of alfalfa. Hot and dry in the summer, the climate here is ideal for the growing of fruits and vegetables.

HILLS OF SAGE slope steeply up from the valley near Keremeos. These parched desert hills contrast sharply with the lush green orchards and fields of the irrigated valley bottom.

THE RICHTER PASS near Cawston. Here Highway No. 3 turns east and climbs over a low ridge of desert hills to the Okanagan Valley.

SPOTTED LAKE along the Richter Pass. This unusual little lake lies in the middle of a rugged desert landscape. It is said that Indian Tribes from hereabouts have been coming here for many years to bathe in its highly mineralized waters claiming that the lake waters have great curative powers.

13

CHRISTINA LAKE is a popular recreational area. Many cottages dot the shores of this beautiful lake which lies along Highway No. 3 near the Kettle River Falls.

HIGHWAY 3 near Grand Forks, is seen at right, as it skirts the dry hills along the banks of the Kettle River west of Christina Lake.

GRAND FORKS is a fascinating little town located at the confluence of the Granby and Kettle Rivers. The south eastern gateway to this region, Grand Forks, is steeped in history and is justly famous for its authentic Russian food. It is often prepared by the descendants of the "Doukhobors"– Russian immigrants that settled the valley many years ago.

THE GRANBY RIVER valley must be one of the most scenic in this region. Even the huge piles of black slag, remnants of bygone smelting activity, which can be seen near Grand Forks, are in their own way starkly beautiful.

15.

A ROCK CREEK HOMESTEAD. Its well-tended old buildings and corral make an interesting rural study in the late afternoon light.

THE TOWN OF GREENWOOD is today, a typical neat country town catering to tourists travelling Highway 3 and a local population mostly involved in ranching and forestry. In days long past however, Greenwood was a thriving centre of mining and smelting activity. Across a small stream from the village, we come upon the awesome ruins of the old smelter. High on a ridge, framed by golden Cottonwoods, and silhouetted against the blue sky, stands a gigantic red brick smoke stack. From where we stand, a huge duct or trough slopes up the hill towards the giant stack, its domed brick roof long ago collapsed. This monstrous structure at one time provided the powerful draft which was needed to operate the "blast furnaces" in which the ore was smelted. Further to the west, almost filling the small valley and stretching for hundreds of yards, lies the old waste or "slag dump". Literally, a mountain of slag has been deposited here. Much of this coal black, glass-like material, remains exactly as it cooled after it had been dumped molten from special rail cars. Some of the slag had apparently been allowed to cool and harden before it was dumped or removed from the slag cars, for these huge chunks of slag now lie helter-skelter; their cluttered broken shapes creating a grotesquely beautiful, almost surreal, landscape.

A RAIL FENCE guards a pasture bright with dandelions along Highway 33 near the village of Beaverdell. This alternate route to the central Okanagan follows the scenic West Kettle River for much of the way.

16

THE ROCK CREEK CANYON BRIDGE provides a lofty short-cut across this deep gorge. This sturdy passage for Highway 3, once had the distinction of being the highest highway bridge in Canada.

ON ANARCHIST MOUNTAIN the highway, after reaching a summit of 3700 feet, dives quickly towards the valley floor and Osoyoos Lake. To maintain an easily negotiable grade, this ribbon of asphalt must now twist and wind and switch back upon itself time and time again. Several viewpoints provide us with spectacular views of the valley below and the Cascade Mountains in the distance.

DESERT SAGE, again becomes the dominant plant cover here. As we pause for a moment to admire the view, we become aware of the golden yellow blossoms, their distinctive perfume blending exquisitely with the clear desert air.

AT BRIDESVILLE the route of Highway 3 takes us over lush fields and farm lands as it meanders purposefully towards the valley of the Okanagan.

THE VILLAGE OF OSOYOOS nestles in the valley bottom along the shores of Osoyoos Lake. This little Okanagan town has a distinctive continental personality. Many of the buildings reflect a Mediterranean influence as does the town hall. Here, Highway No. 3 joins the international Highway No. 97 which enters the Okanagan Valley at the busy Canada/U.S.A. border crossing, just south of the Village of Osoyoos.

19

OSOYOOS LAKE, shown here, is the warmest fresh water lake in Canada with an average summer temperature of 21 °C. The lake, with its many miles of safe sandy beaches, is a popular vacation spot for summer visitors. Accommodations are excellent, ranging from campgrounds to luxurious condominiums.

FRUIT GROWING, in this the most southern of Okanagan communities, ranks even higher in importance than tourism. The two industries, however, compliment each other. Many visitors come to Osoyoos each summer, first to enjoy the sights and the aroma of blossomtime, then later, to share in the succulent bounty of sun ripened Okanagan fruit.

Osoyoos and district is one of the important soft fruit growing areas in Canada. Thousands of tons of cherries, plums, peaches, nectarines, apricots, and a host of other soft fruits are packed and shipped each year to major centres in Canada and abroad.

Osoyoos is situated at the southern most end of the Okanagan Valley and enjoys a warm, dry climate. Summer comes early here allowing the fruit growers of this community to harvest and ship the earliest fruit available in Canada.

"CANADA'S VEST POCKET DESERT" is the way in which this area is often described. Receiving an average rainfall of less than 8 inches per year, the sage covered sandy plains and hills hereabouts harbor a variety of desert plants and animals. An excellent example of this Okanagan desert country, still undisturbed, can be seen on the east side of Osoyoos Lake.

20

GRAPE GROWERS AND WINE MAKERS together have transformed large tracts of this desert country between Oliver and Osoyoos into lush productive vineyards. The climate here, comparable to California's Napa Valley and the fine grape growing regions of France and Germany, produces grapes of exceptional wine making quality. Such well known names as Brights Wines, Casabello Wines, Gehringer Brothers, Okanagan Vineyards, LeComte Estate, Divino Estate, St. Laslo Vineyards, and Sumac Ridge are on the labels of many fine wines produced from grapes grown here in this south Okanagan region.

Tours and tastings are offered by all of the major wineries as well as many of the smaller estate wineries. These tours are delightful and provide the visitor with an opportunity to taste some of the fine wines that are made in these south Okanagan communities.

Many of the wineries operate wine shops where visitors may purchase their favourite variety. Each winery features it's own special labels, including, Okanagan Riesling, Chardonnay, Gewurztraminer, Burgundy, Chablis, and other classic types. Some of the wineries offer gift packs, holding two or three bottles attractively packaged in elegant wooden boxes.

On your next visit, make a point to attend a winery tour and tasting; You will be pleasantly surprised and delighted.

THE IRRIGATION CANALS of Oliver, are one of the scenic wonders that can be seen throughout this fruit growing community. These canals originate upstream on the Okanagan River where the water is diverted at an "intake", then distributed by a system of flumes, siphons, and canals throughout the lush orchards of the area.

PICKING APPLES in his orchard at Oliver, a grower is shown here using a "Girette" which is a mechanized portable platform with an extendible boom or arm that can be raised, lowered, and moved from side to side by the operator as required. This area is noted for the production of fine fruits and vegetables; in particular, great quantities of high quality apples, grapes, and melons are harvested each year.

THE TOWN OF OLIVER serves this land of sunshine and fruit. Many buildings along the main street reflect a sturdy pioneering quality reminiscent of Oliver's colourful and historic past. In sharp contrast, is the modern hospital shown here. Oliver hosts many visitors each year and offers some excellent accommodation and services. The airport, with a newly surfaced 3,200 foot run-way and new terminal building, is within walking distance of the downtown and major shopping centre.

MCINTIRE MOUNTAIN, shown here beyond a tawny field of range grass framed by a group of Ponderosa Pine trees, creates a picture that is typical of the rugged south Okanagan countryside surrounding Oliver.

24

THE MOUNT BALDY ski area is located 35 km east of Oliver and boasts of sunshine and powder snow. The mountain stands approximately 7,580 feet high. Its symetric snow-capped peak is a landmark and can be seen from miles around. Here a group of trees, branches heavily laden with snow and frost, guard this powdery winter wonderland.

A DOWNHILL SKIER is seen here enjoying Baldy's slopes. A 4800 ft. T-bar lift moves skiers quickly to the top. The ski lift, cafeteria and lounge are generally open from mid November to early May.

CROSS-COUNTRY SKIING is popular at the Mount Baldy ski area. Here a group of cross country skiers pause for a moment to enjoy the scenic winter view.

AN OKANAGAN SKI PICNIC without Okanagan wine is like a day without sunshine. An old adage, with which these two attractive lady skiers obviously agree, as they pause to enjoy the Okanagan sunshine and a cold crisp bottle of Okanagan wine.

PONDEROSA PINE TREES stand on a ridge silhouetted against the blue Okanagan sky.

SEEING THE INVISIBLE. These enormous radio antennas are part of a research facility located at the White Lake basin near Okanagan Falls. These antennas at the Dominion Radio Astrophysical Observatory can "see" beyond the range of visible light. Here astronomers from the National Research Council position and aim these antennas to pick up radio signals emanating from outer space. Analyzing and interpreting such signals is part of the science of radio astronomy. Canada has two such observatories, the other being in Algonquin Park in Ontario. During daylight hours a unique and interesting self-guided tour is offered to visitors by the observatory.

THE WHITE LAKE BASIN, where the observatory is located, is a broad, dry, sage covered valley surrounded by rugged mountains. The site is ideal as the air is clean and clear assuring excellent visibility. The high mountain ridges shield the area from unwanted radio interference. This view overlooks the basin to the west.

VASEAUX LAKE is located north of Oliver along Highway 97 and is part of the Okanagan River system. A bird and wildlife sanctuary, Vaseaux is home to many species of waterfowl. California big horn sheep are often seen along the rugged shoreline.

MACINTIRE BLUFF, a famous local landmark, is seen here reflecting in the calm waters of Vaseaux Lake.

OKANAGAN FALLS is the traditional meeting place of local ranchers. Located at the south end of Skaha Lake, this little town is surrounded by rugged Okanagan Mountains, which can be seen in the distance.

OKANAGAN APPLE BLOSSOMS attract many visitors each year to the Kaleden district which is noted for its fine apples as well as soft fruits. Generally, apple blossom time occurs in early May. At this time, the hillside orchards of Kaleden burst into a profusion of white and pink apple blossoms, their fragrance permeating the warm spring air. In a few short months, these same trees will be laden with plump apples, crisp and sweet. We promise to return at harvest time so that we may enjoy some of the luscious fruits that these Kaleden orchardists will be offering.

Perhaps upon our return we will take some time to visit the Okanagan Game Farm which houses hundreds of species of animals from all over the world. It is located at Kaleden, just across the highway from our favourite fruit stand.

CHANNEL DRIFTING in the Okanagan River between Okanagan and Skaha Lake, is an increasingly popular activity. Each summer, thousands of enthusiastic kids, young and old, can be found floating leisurely down Penticton's scenic river channel. Here, we catch a glimpse of several enthusiastic channel drifters: each displaying their own special form and technique.

SKAHA LAKE, seen here beyond a sage covered valley, is part of the Okanagan River system. Skaha's clean, warm water is ideal for water sports and it attracts thousands of visitors each summer.

THE CITY OF BEACHES AND
PEACHES is the way Penticton is
often described. Surrounded by
orchards and expansive beaches, the
City of Penticton is the major urban
centre of the South Okanagan.
Although fine tree fruits of all kinds
are grown here, Penticton prides
itself in being known as the "Peach
City". This sweet succulent fruit is
celebrated with great delight each
year by residents and visitors alike.
In Penticton, the festivities begin
each year with blossom time and
continue throughout the spring and
summer culminating with the annual
Penticton Peach Festival during the
last weeks of July. Indeed, peach
season is definitely very special in
Penticton.

WADING IN THE SPARKLING
SURF, a sun bronzed young visitor
enjoys the warm crystal clear waters
of one of Penticton's safe, sandy
beaches.

PENTICTON BEACHES are a
source of civic pride. Located between
the two lakes, Penticton boasts of
broad, clean expansive beaches on
both Okanagan and Skaha Lake.

OKANAGAN PEACHES, sweet
and delightful, here being enthusias-
tically enjoyed by two charming
young ladies, who themselves, might
aptly be described in similar terms.
Baskets of fine luscious fruit, laugh-
ter, sunshine, warm clear water on a
fine sandy beach, are some of the
elements that contribute to an exciting vacation here in this wonderful
city of "Beaches and Peaches"

35

THE PENTICTON TRADE AND CONVENTION CENTRE welcomes thousands of conventioneers each year. The newly renovated facility, shown here is, the largest of its kind in western Canada. Staffed by full time convention experts, this facility offers complete convention services to meetings ranging in size from 20 to 6,000 delegates. The city of Penticton may indeed take pride in this fine convention centre.

THE PENTICTON INTERNATIONAL AIRPORT is conveniently located on the west edge of the city. The airport is an international port of entry and offers customs and immigration services. Flights to and from Vancouver, Calgary and other B.C. cities visit the Penticton airport daily.

THE CITY OF PENTICTON bills itself as the "hospitality capital of Canada". Indeed, this south Okanagan city does play host to thousands of visitors each year offering excellent accommodation, shopping and restaurant facilities. A host of annual activities make Penticton a favourite holiday destination. The Blossom Festival, the British Columbia Square Dance Jamboree, the Penticton Peach Festival and the Iron Man Canada Triathlon, are but a few of the exciting events that Penticton plays host to each year.

THE DELTA LAKESIDE HOTEL, shown here, is a fine example of the luxurious and elegant accommodations that are available in the City of Penticton.

37

CONTEMPORARY ARCHITEC-TURE is evident in many of Penticton's most recently construct-ed buildings. Here, we see an elegant lakeside condominium which offers the discriminating buyer a luxurious lifestyle.

MANY GOVERNMENT OFFICES are located in Penticton including the area office for Revenue Canada. Here, we see the facade of the Provincial Government building located on Skaha Road.

THE RETIRED SENIORS CENTRE, shown here, is only one of the senior citizen's retirement projects established in Penticton.

THE PENTICTON REGIONAL HOSPITAL, shown here, is a fine medical facility which provides a wide range of hospital services to the city of Penticton and the South Okanagan region.

THE PENTICTON ART GALLERY is located on the shores of Okanagan Lake. Recently completed, this contemporary solar heated building houses local, regional, national, and international exhibitions.

PENTICTON'S COMMUNITY CENTRE is a modern multipurpose facility. The building houses a theatre and an aquatics area, a gymnasium, and a fitness room. There are several racquetball courts, a dance studio, and three indoor tennis courts.

40

ORCHARDS AND VINEYARDS cover the hillsides around Penticton. Fertile benchlands extend south to Okanagan Falls and north to Naramata and Summerland. On these warm sandy hillsides growers produce tons of tree fruits and grapes each year helping to support a thriving packing, shipping and processing industry.

OKANAGAN TIMBER is the raw material that fuels the forest industry in Penticton. Weyerhaeuser Canada Limited operates a large mill in Okanagan Falls, Greenwood Forest Products a smaller one in town. Logs are hauled to the Weyerhaeuser operation from forest areas as far north as the Greystoke Plateau and from as far south as the Canada-U.S.A. border.

TWO OKANAGAN WINERIES using locally grown grapes are located in Penticton and Summerland. Casabello Wines in downtown Penticton , the oldest and the largest, bottles a wide variety of wines under several well known Okanagan labels. Sumac Ridge Estate Winery is located in Summerland. It produces several distinctive wines including classic Gewürztraminer and Okanagan Riesling. Both of these Wineries welcome visitors for tours and tastings. Wine may be purchased at their wine shops.

MANUFACTURING is growing in importance. Farm machinery, plastics, mobile homes, metal, wood and a host of other products are made in Penticton.

OKANAGAN FRUIT, of the finest quality, is grown here in the South Okanagan. On the left a colorful group of pictures illustrate the wide variety of fine fruit that is grown in and around Penticton.

FROZEN WHITE SENTINALS *seen on the facing page mark the timberline near Apex Alpine's wind-blown summit. Trees and snags, covered in snow and frost and bent by the wind, form these coldly beautiful shapes which are shown here silhouetted against the deep blue Okanagan sky.*

APEX ALPINE, *located approximately 30 kilometers west of Penticton, offers a full range of services and accommodation to the avid skier. The mountain maintains many groomed runs to delight the beginner and the confident intermediate skier. At the same time, boasting of 2,000 vertical feet, Apex has terrain that will challenge the most accomplished expert.*

THE APEX ALPINE VILLAGE, *shown at left, includes a cluster of condominiums, shops, restaurants and bars as well as a day lodge and cafeteria.*

APEX ALPINE *is noted for dry powder snow and Okanagan Sunshine. Skiers come from far and wide to ski the sunny slopes of this South Okanagan mountain. Here, on the left, a group of skiers flash down a groomed slope near the Lodge at Apex Alpine.*

FAMILY SKIING FUN *is featured at Apex Alpine. Here we see three sturdy youngsters preparing to ascend the mountain.*

SNOWBOARDING, *although relatively new, is fast becoming a popular winter sport. Here, displaying fine form, we see a youngster flash across the hill.*

43

THE SS SICAMOUS, the last of the great sternwheelers, now rests aground at Riverside Park in Penticton. She was launched at Okanagan Landing in 1914 and it was rumoured she had cost an incredible $180,000. Her steel hull was of a new design featuring water tight compartments. It is said that she could carry 500 passengers with a full compliment of luggage, plus assorted freight, and still make a very acceptable 17 knots. On her maiden voyage the Sicamous was welcomed with great excitement by crowds of cheering people at her various calling places along Okanagan Lake; Carrs Landing, Ewings Landing, Caesar's Landing, and Wilsons Landing were but a few of the small Okanagan communities that she regularly visited. She was indeed a magnificent and elegant lady. Her fittings were of polished brass, she had great plate glass mirrors and skylights of colourful stained glass, comfortable enclosed observation decks and a huge elegant dining room. An old timer recalls, "The service was splendid and the food, excellent". Today, the Sicamous no longer plies the waters of Okanagan Lake having been set to rest here many years ago. Her thundering paddle wheel is now silent and still. We feel a certain sadness as we walk her deserted passageways and peer into her empty pilot house. She seems forlorn indeed. As we take our leave down the well-trodden gangway, we wish, with a backward glance, that this proud ship could somehow slip her moorings, sound a mighty blast upon her whistle, then cast off, and be once again, the Queen of the Okanagan.

RIVERSIDE PARK now deserted on this cool autumn afternoon.

THE GREAT CLAY CLIFFS of Naramata and Penticton. These great bluffs and mesas stand guard along the southern shores of Okanagan Lake.

THE SUMMERLAND RESEARCH
STATION overlooking Okanagan Lake at
Trout Creek was established in 1914. This
facility is often referred to by the old timers as
the Summerland Experimental Farm. Located
in the centre of the fruit growing area of the
Okanagan Valley, its research program is
designed primarily to serve the grape and tree
fruit industry.

The Summerland station occupies approximately 800 acres with 220 acres under irrigation. About 125 acres are planted with various
tree fruits and grapes. Research programs
being carried out here include studies in ento-
mology, plant pathology, food processing,
pomology, viticulture, soil science and agriculture engineering.

The research station maintains a special ornamental picnic area. Although not part of the
regular research program, this ornamental
area is famous for its beauty and annually
attracts many visitors. Facilities are provided
for picnickers in an enclosed log cabin as well
as at outdoor tables and benches. The picnic
area is open for the convenience of visitors
from 7:30 a.m. to 8:30 p.m., seven days a week
from May 1 to October 31 in each year. The
Summerland Research Station is operated by
the Research Branch of Agriculture Canada.

OKANAGAN LAKE panorama as seen from
the Research Station as Summerland.

SUN-OKA BEACH AT TROUT CREEK is a
favourite with many boaters. A large section of
this beautiful sandy beach is designated and
reserved for boaters and water skiers. On this
sunny afternoon, a family enjoys their
Okanagan summer vacation while on the
beach, two less adventurous visitors eat their
picnic lunch while watching the water skiing
activities.

OKANAGAN LAKE Provincial Campground and Picnic Site located on Highway 97 near Peachland offers excellent lakeside camping and picnic sites to the summer traveller. This fine panoramic view of Okanagan Lake is seen from one of the many hiking trails.

OKANAGAN SAND ROSES, blossoms of the Bitter Root or Spatlum , can be seen along the rocky ridges and sandy glades in early summer.

SQUALLY POINT shown here, and rugged Wild Horse Canyon, are part of the Okanagan Mountain Park located on the east side of Okanagan Lake directly across from the Town of Peachland. The park is easily accessible by boat and is a favourite with naturalists, hikers, and mountaineers.

BALSAM ROOT SUNFLOWERS bloom early in the spring covering the Okanagan hills with a carpet of yellow blossoms.

MANY MOUNTAIN LAKES *are located on the nearby high plateaus. Most of these are water reservoirs and are easily accessible by four-wheel drive vehicle or a short walk on foot. Access to some of these lakes is restricted but several can be reached by float plane. Here we see a flying fisherman trying his luck at Pinaus Lake.*

LOCH LOST *on the Greystoke plateau welcomes a party of four fishermen hikers, its blue waters sparkle invitingly in the early morning light.*

A CATCH *of Rainbow Trout, shown at left, is the ultimate reward and is the prize that these fishermen pursue. Trout will take trolled lures as well as wet and dry flies.*

BLUE GROUSE *are plentiful and are often seen on these high mountain plateaus.*

OKANAGAN LAKE, *viewed from the Westside Road near Kelowna is seen here in the spring when the grassy hillsides turn golden with a profusion of glowing Balsam Root Sunflowers. The Westside Road is a scenic alternate route north. Bear Creek Provincial Campground, a popular westside Kelowna campsite, is located along this route. Other scenic attractions include Bear Creek Canyon, Bear Lake and Wilson's Landing. Here too, we can visit Okanagan Lake Resort which offers a full range of water sports , fine dining, golf, tennis, hiking, and horseback riding. A fine choice for an Okanagan holiday.*

THE OKANAGAN LAKE BRIDGE *at Kelowna, opened in 1958, is Canada's largest floating bridge structure. Its floating span is comprised of twelve separate concrete pontoons which were fastened together end-to-end, to form a floating roadbed over 2,000 feet in length. This huge floating structure is held in place by 24 gigantic concrete anchors similar to one that is displayed in a small park alongside the highway in the City of Kelowna. The Okanagan Lake Bridge steel structure spans more than 600 feet and has four girdered steel structures. One of these, the large centre section, spans 265 feet between two concrete piers which rest on the lake bottom. This centre span can be raised to a clearance of 60 feet to allow larger ship traffic to pass through.*
The Okanagan Lake bridge provides a passage for Highway 97 across Okanagan Lake at Kelowna. Prior to 1958 a fleet of car ferries provided the Highway 97 link. Since then, however, this bridge has become a landmark of the City of Kelowna. The car ferries have been retired with the exception of one which has been converted to a riverboat style stern wheeler. Named the "Fintry Queen" this unique vessel has itself become a Kelowna legend.

53

"THE SPIRIT OF SAIL" is the name that was given to this famous Kelowna landmark by its creator, Okanagan artist and sculptor, R. (Bob) Dow-Reid. More commonly known as "The Sails", this elegant sculpture was erected October 18, 1977. Fashioned of fiberglass at the R. Dow-Reid studio on Lakeshore Road, it was later transported to the site by helicopter. 38 Feet high and weighing 3,400 pounds, Bob Dow-Reid recalls "It's a good thing it wasn't a bit bigger because the ship that Okanagan Helicopters used to transport the piece could only lift 4,000 pounds."

Originally erected in 1973 by the City of Kelowna, this fountain was to be known as the "Pioneer Fountain" in honour of Kelowna's pioneers, in particular a tribute to one of Kelowna's most famous pioneers, Mr. Pasquale (Cap) Capozzi, D.B.A. Kerry Park at the foot of Bernard Avenue, where this tribute to the pioneers was erected, is but a stone's throw from many places of business that were established by Kelowna's old timers. Names like Bennett, Capozzi, Raymer, Whillis, and Ritchie are but a few that we recall with fondness. We can be sure that these men of vision would be pleased if they could somehow share in our sense of enjoyment as we behold Kelowna's beautiful fountain of "The Sails".

THE LEGEND OF OGOPOGO is retold many times here on the shores of Lake Okanagan. The friendly creature who is said to inhabit the lake, Ogopogo, was first seen by the native Indians. They called him by a name which sounded like "N'ha-a'itk" which, roughly translated, means, "creature of the water" or "lake demon". Many sightings describing a strange creature similar to this replica have been reported throughout the years. These sightings, which occur mostly in the summer, would seem to prove that a creature does exist and inhabits Okanagan Lake. As he is seen near here most often, legend has it that Ogopogo lives in an under-water cave near Kelowna.

THE CITY HALL of Kelowna is the centre-piece of an administrative core area comprising several blocks which include the Provincial Government Courthouse, the R.C.M.P. Headquarters Building, the Kelowna Community Theatre, the Memorial Arena, the Museum-Art Gallery, and the Regional Health Centre. A clock tower fountain, dedicated to the memory of the Honourable W.A.C. Bennett, a former Premier of the Province of British Columbia, dominates a small square next to a charming Japanese Garden, which recognizes the city of Kasugai in Japan, Kelowna's adopted sister city.

KELOWNA COMMUNITY THEATRE, seen here, will soon be renovated to create a larger and more contemporary theatre complex.

THE KELOWNA CITY PARK provides a shady retreat for residents and visitors alike. Seen here, the park features seasonal floral displays including the beautiful "Rose Garden". Kelowna's famous "Hot Sands Beach" on Okanagan Lake is part of the City Park.

THE KELOWNA MUSEUM BUILDING is soon to become part of a new and exciting Museum-Art Gallery and exhibition complex which is proposed for the site.

THE KELOWNA GENERAL HOSPITAL is slated to undergo another major expansion and renovation. Providing medical services to the people of the entire Central Okanagan region, this modern hospital offers many up-to-date diagnostic, surgical, and other medical treatment facilities.

THE CAPRI HOTEL and shopping centre complex is centrally located in Kelowna. It offers residents and visitors luxurious accommodations, exciting entertainment, and fine dining.

THE EXECUTIVE HOUSE, at left, provides its occupants with a prestigious address, luxury, and security at a central downtown location.

ORCHARD PARK SHOPPING CENTRE is located near the geographic centre of the city. Attracting shoppers from throughout the Okanagan region, Orchard Park is the largest shopping mall in the Okanagan Valley. At right, the entrance to the South Mall beckons us to enter, stroll the wide climate controlled concourse as we enjoy shopping at the Orchard Park Mall.

THE CITY OF KELOWNA is the largest city in the Okanagan Valley. Located on a broad valley plain, Kelowna lies neatly along the sandy shores of Okanagan Lake and is surrounded by the lush apple orchards and vineyards for which this area is justly famous. Long, hot summers and mild winters here have made Kelowna a favourite vacation and retirement centre. Enjoying more than 2,000 hours of sunshine annually, Kelowna attracts thousands of visitors each year. Many of these will resolve to retire here.

A RETIRED SENIORS RESIDENCE is shown at left. This impressive project is operated under the auspices of the Kelowna Kiwanis Club.

MEDICAL AND DENTAL services are offered by various medical practitioners who share this contemporary Kelowna building with two spacious movie theatres.

THE BLOSSOM TIME SAILING REGATTA is held at Kelowna each year. This exciting annual event draws sailors from far and wide. Generally held on the third weekend in May, this Regatta coincides with apple blossom time in Kelowna. It is at this time each year that the surrounding hillside apple orchards burst into a dazzling display of beautifully delicate and fragrant blossoms.

WATER SPORTS at Kelowna are a favourite summer pastime. Residents and visitors, young and old alike, are not content to just lay about on the beautiful sandy beaches. Everyone, it seems, wants to get into the swim, so to speak. Here, we see a colorful mosaic of exciting activity. A charming water skier adjusts her harness while a companion flashes across the sparkling waves. Windsurfers take advantage of a sudden squall or chat waiting on the beach for the wind to rise. A pretty sailer checks the halyard on her hobycat while a delighted tuber skims across a foaming wake. Along the sandy shore, a ride on a fun island delights a laughing youngster and his attractive mom.

CANADA'S FAMOUS SNOW BIRDS precision flying team performs at the Kelowna International Regatta.

KELOWNA AT DUSK is seen here from one of the view points in Knox Mountain Park.

AQUATIC COMPETITIONS featuring enthusiastic local teams are often scheduled as part of various water festival and Regatta events.

REGATTAS AND SUMMER FESTIVALS are staged each year in the city of Kelowna and surrounding districts. Very popular are the Knox Mountain Hill Climb, Rutland May Days, the Blossom Time Sailing Regatta, Westside Days, the Kelowna International Regatta, Folkfest, and Lake Country Days, to name just a few. Special events are featured by Sunshine Theatre throughout the whole summer while in the fall the Okanagan Wine Festival stages many events including displays, wine tastings, and the exciting wine stomp competitions.

BOAT RACES are always a popular part of the Regatta and water festival events.

WATER SKIING championships are often held at Kelowna. Here, we see Kelowna's Bobby Jones perform a graceful cut.

THE MV FINTRY QUEEN, Kelowna's famous paddlewheeler, is popular for its sightseeing and evening dinner cruises.

KELOWNA, "THE APPLE CAPITAL OF CANADA" is a phrase often used to describe this Okanagan city. Above, a sturdy youngster munches happily on one of Kelowna's finest, a crisp, sweet McIntosh. On the facing page, a fine display of Kelowna Red Delicious.

66

FRUIT AND TIMBER are the raw materials that drive Kelowna's industrial economy. In recent years, however, manufacturing and service industries have grown in importance.

B.C. TREE FRUITS LTD., the central selling agency for the B.C. Fruit Growers Association, is headquartered in Kelowna along with several of the valley's largest fruit packing plants. Sun-Rype Products, the growers' processing division, operates a large modern plant at Kelowna where it produces the world famous "Sun-Rype Apple Juice" and other fruit products including, various fruit nectars and pie fillings. Visitors are welcome.

KELOWNA AND DISTRICT WINERIES, produce from local grapes, a wide variety of excellent wines. Calona Wines is Kelowna's oldest, largest, and most awarded winery. The other of the large commercial wineries is Mission Hill Vineyards located in Westbank. It too, is much awarded and claims the most scenic location. Chateau Ste. Claire, Gray Monk Cellars, and Cedar Creek Estate are three of the smaller estate wineries which are established here. The wineries all welcome visitors and offer tours and tastings. Wines are available for sale at their wine shops.

THE FOREST INDUSTRY at Kelowna is led by Crown Forest Industries Ltd. which operates several large plants manufacturing lumber, plywood, and containers. Crown Forest and Gorman Brothers in Westbank, together, receive logs from throughout the area and support an extensive logging industry.

MANUFACTURING AND PROCESSING are led by Western Star Trucks Ltd. and Hiram Walker Okanagan Distillery. Western Star, in downtown Kelowna, employs more than 500 people, and is engaged in the manufacturing of heavy duty Class 8 trucks. Hiram Walker, has a large plant in Winfield where it makes many different brands of liquor including the internationally famous "Canadian Club Whiskey". "Three Buoys Houseboats" and "Okanagan" brand recreational vehicles are manufactured in Kelowna as well. Many of these industrial plants welcome visitors.

THE KELOWNA-VERNON INTERNATIONAL AIRPORT is the major airport for the Okanagan Valley. Scheduled flights service Vancouver, Calgary, Edmonton, and other major cities. The airport is home base to Kelowna Flightcraft Air Charter, one of Kelowna's fastest growing industries. Internationally recognized as a leading overhaul and repair facility for larger aircraft, Kelowna Flightcraft lists the Canadian government as one of its largest customers. In addition, they are one of Canada's largest air carriers, operating their own fleet of 727's and 580 Convairs moving tons of parcel freight across Canada daily for Purolator Courier Service.

THE OKANAGAN COLLEGE *is a community-oriented college with campuses located at Penticton, Kelowna, Vernon and Salmon Arm. This Okanagan Post-Secondary Institution provides a unique opportunity to all the people of this region both young and old alike, to acquire an advanced education. The Kelowna campus seen here on the right is the administrative center and has the largest number of students in attendance. Okanagan College offers a wide range of courses to a diverse student population. Because of the multiple campuses many young people are able to live at home while they attend classes. As a result of a concerted drive by the community over the past several years, the status of Okanagan College has been recently elevated to that of a degree-granting University.*

THE FATHER PANDOSY MISSION *shown at right is an interesting historic site located at Kelowna. This little Mission was established in 1859 by the Reverend Father Charles Pandosy and several other members of the oblate order of Mary Immaculate. This Roman Catholic mission was the first on the mainland of British Columbia. Father Pandosy, his oblate brothers, and their few followers built a small mission enclave near the banks of what is now Mission Creek. They planted a small orchard, which as it happens, marked the beginning of the fruit industry in the Okanagan Valley. Father Pandosy spent 30 years in the Okanagan helping his flock, saying mass, teaching school and music. The good Father died in 1891 at the age of 67.*

Thanks to the efforts of the Okanagan Historical Society and others, this fascinating heritage site still stands today. This historical site is open to the public daily from 8:00 a.m. to dusk, seven days a week. There are picnic tables, so pack your lunch when you plan to visit. The Father Pandosy Mission is located on Benvoulin Road in Kelowna.

KELOWNA GOLF COURSES are internationally famous and challenge the skill of the most accomplished professional as well as the Sunday afternoon duffer. The prestigious and beautiful Kelowna Golf & Country Club and the challenging Gallagher's Canyon Golf Resort courses are the two that are the most well known. The Canadian Junior Men's Golf Championship has been hosted by the Kelowna Golf & Country Club while the Canadian Amateur Golf Championship was played at Gallagher's Canyon. Seven other golf course are established in the Kelowna area and offer golfers a wide range of challenging terrain. These are the Central Park Golf Course, the Mission Creek Golf Course, the Fairview Golf Course, and executive layout, and the Shadow Ridge Golf Course in Kelowna, the Shannon Lake Golf Course in Westbank, the Ponderosa Golf & Country Club with its spectacular panoramic view of Okanagan Lake located in Peachland, and the Aspen Grove Golf Club executive layout in Winfield. Each of these scenic Okanagan Golf Courses offer a unique golfing experience to professionals and amateurs alike.

THE KELOWNA GOLF & COUNTRY CLUB was established in 1920 and occupies a beautiful site very close to downtown Kelowna surrounding a natural pond located at the foot of Dilworth Mountain. A modern clubhouse offers a panoramic view of Eagle Pond and the scenic Dilworth Mountain bluffs. The challenging course layout occupies more than a 120 acres and is designed that each hole is well separated from adjoining fairways. Stately old Ponderosa Pines as well as other strategically placed trees provide the natural hazards as does Eagle Pond, the central water way.

EAGLE POND is the central scenic feature and water hazard at the Kelowna Golf & Country Club. At right, we see the Clubhouse overlooking the pond, which is inhabited by the club mascots, a pair of stately black swans.

GALLAGHER'S CANYON GOLF RESORT, shown at left, is located in East Kelowna. Opened in June of 1980 this sprawling 18-hole layout offers a tremendous golfing challenge. Its long tight fairways and gracefully undulating greens require extraordinary shot-making skills. Skirting the edge of spectacular Gallagher's Canyon, this golf course ranks with the finest when compared as to scenic beauty . Once the site of the Canadian Amateur Golf Championship, this beautiful course with it's long pine-fringed fairways and beautiful setting provides an exciting challenge to visiting professionals and dedicated amateurs alike.

A SNOW DRAGON extends a gloved hand in greeting. Trees bent and heavily laden with snow and frost form the twisted white shape which resembles a friendly snow dragon extending a white gloved hand. We imagine that this friendly snow dragon might be saying "Welcome All Yee Skiers to Big White".

RIDING THE CHAIR LIFT, a group of happy skiers are seen here enjoying their return trip to the top of the ski runs.

SKI OKANAGAN and enjoy sparkling winter sunshine and powder snow. Ski at Last Mountain near Kelowna which offers excellent groomed slopes and night skiing, or at Big White, Kelowna's famous mountain of powder. These two Okanagan Ski Resorts offer terrain and conditions to suit the taste of everyone.

"Big White", shown here, is the highest in elevation and features lots of sunshine and dry powder snow, with 44 downhill runs and more than 10 miles of groomed cross-country trails. Big White has, on the mountain, overnight accommodation for more than 2400 skiers ranging from cozy hotel rooms to spacious and luxurious condominium suites. Seven ski lifts provide uphill transportation while numerous hotels, restaurants and pubs, offer exciting aprés ski dining and entertainment.

THREE BIG WHITE SKIERS pause to enjoy the exhilarating view before plunging once again down the challenging slopes.

THE MOUNTAIN OF POWDER is a very appropriate description of Kelowna's Big White. Here we see an attractive lady skier who has quite literally lost herself in her enjoyment of the fluffy powder snow.

A FLOAT PLANE *rides gently aground on a sparkling Kalamalka Lake beach. This form of aerial sightseeing is indeed a thrilling way to enjoy Kalamalka and many of the other spectacular lakes of the Okanagan.*

KALAMALKA LAKE, *seen here, is one sparkling emerald jewel in a chain of three lakes that border Highway 97's scenic route from Kelowna to Vernon. Duck Lake, just north of the Kelowna-Vernon International Airport, formerly the site of the Canadian Water Ski Championships, is the first scenic jewel in this chain. Wood Lake, just north of the community of Winfield and south of Oyama, forms the second jewel. A more vivid shade of turquoise, the clean, clear waters of this lake attract many summer visitors. Wood lake is the focal point of interest and activity when these communities stage "Lake Country Days", their annual summer festival. Farther to the north lies Kalamalka Lake, the third jewel, even more spectacular and beautiful in its colouring. Shades of blue, green, and turquoise in ever changing hues make Lake Kalamalka a scenic extravaganza which surely deserves the name ,"Lake of Many Colours".*

KALAMALKA LAKE *is noted for it's clear sparkling turquoise blue waters. Along it's many fine beaches hundreds of happy summer visitors play in the Okanagan sunshine. At left, on a more secluded beach near Cousins Bay, we see two delightful Okanagan beauties as they wade into the clear sparkling waters of Kalamalka Lake.*

THE TUG NARAMATA is seen here at her resting place at Okanagan Landing. This sturdy ship is the last of the coal burning steam tugs that once plied the waters of Okanagan Lake. The Naramata, formerly a C.P.R. tug, was used for many years to move heavy barges laden with railcars that carried timber, cattle, apples, and other produce to market.

PARA-SAILING, a visitor soars high above the lake as he is towed behind a speed boat. Para-sailing on Okanagan Lake is a popular and thrilling summertime activity.

BOATING ON THE OKANAGAN is a favourite with summer visitors. Hundreds of miles of scenic shoreline make Okanagan Lake the choice of many boaters. Scenic spots like Quarry Bay and Otter Bay are located near Vernon. Here, an attractive Okanagan boater waves a friendly greeting near Otter Bay in Ellison Park .

OKANAGAN LANDING lies south of Vernon on the northeast arm of Okanagan Lake. At right, we catch a glimpse of this north Okanagan Community as we seem to skim across the clear blue waters of Okanagan lake.

WINDSURFING, sailing, swimming, boating, and just plain sun-tanning on the beach are some of the activities that we might enjoy if we were to vacation in this area. At left, a pretty Okanagan windsurfer prepares to ride the wind over the sparkling waves.

THE VERNON COURT HOUSE, shown on the right, stands on a hill overlooking the town. The court house is constructed of native granite quarried on the shores of Okanagan Lake at what is now called Quarry Bay. This fine old building still serves as the major hall of justice for the city of Vernon and the Okanagan Valley.

THE VERNON CITY HALL is the centrepiece of a complex that includes several civic buildings. Some of the buildings are shown here on the left. The City Hall buildings are grouped around small squares, gardens, and fountains, which form a most attractive civic centre complex.

THE VERNON MUSEUM AND ARCHIVES, shown on the left, is part of the civic centre. Displaying Indian arrowheads, baskets, and many other artifacts which recall the history of the north Okanagan, the archives are an important link to Vernon's past history and native culture. The Topham-Brown Art Gallery showing local artists as well as travelling exhibitions is also located in the Vernon Civic Centre.

THE CITY OF VERNON is situated at the top of the beautiful Okanagan Valley and like it's neighboring Okanagan cities is noted for it's fine climate and warm hospitality. Forestry, agriculture, manufacturing and tourism are the mainstays of Vernon's economy.

THE MALL at Village Green, Vernon's modern shopping centre at left, serves the residents of this city and the north Okanagan.

POLSON PARK shown at right in brilliant autumn dress. This lovely downtown park is popular with residents and visitors alike. This civic park is famous for its displays of flowers in the great floral clock of Polson Park.

THE VERNON JUBILEE HOSPITAL, shown on the left, provides a full range of medical services to the people of Vernon and the North Okanagan. This handsome building of contemporary modern design, contrasts sharply with some of Vernon's beautiful old buildings shown on the right.

THE NATIONAL HOTEL was originally built in 1905 by a man named Rueben Swift. "The Royal Hotel", as it was then called, stands on it's original site today hiding behind a flamboyant lower facade which was added in 1971 by the late Max Fishler. Rueben Swift, the original builder of this brick building, was a colorful and popular figure. He served as a city alderman from 1905 to 1910. A keen sportsman, he is remembered as the father of cricket in the Okanagan. Max Fishler, like his predecessor, was also a popular Vernon citizen and himself an enthusiastic booster of sports. The original cost of this colorful historical building was a staggering $20,000.

THE LAND & AGRICULTURE BUILDING, shown here on the right, was originally built in 1911 at a cost of $5,000. This beautiful brick building, with it's columnar gabled balastrade, is a classic example of an elegant office building in the architectural style of it's time.

THE OLD VERNON RAILROAD STATION, shown on the lower right, is remarkably well preserved. This sturdy building brings back fond memories of huge puffing steam locomotives and elegant railroad cars. Of the stern conductor dressed in blue serge consulting his railroad watch, then turning to shout, "All Aboard."

THE KALAMALKA CENTER of Okanagan College, shown here on the left, reflects the contemporary architectural style of the 80's. The Vernon campus of Okanagan College serves the people of this area providing first and second year university, vocational, and a wide variety of community educational courses.

85

SILVER STAR MOUNTAIN is located just north of Vernon. As we see at left, this winter wonderland is enjoyed by both skiers and snowmobilers. Although laid out and kept apart, facilities for both these winter activities are provided on the mountain.

THE VILLAGE AT SILVER STAR is one of Western Canada's favorite ski destinations. Shown on the right, are some of the hotels and saloons that are part of this charming mountaintop village.

THE VERNON WINTER CARNIVAL held each year at the beginning of February is a joyous celebration of the many activities that are so much a part of the winter scene in Vernon. This exciting festival features winter sporting events and many cultural and community activities. Indeed, winter carnival is an exciting time in Vernon.

THE SUMMIT OF SILVER STAR, shown on the right, is incredibly beautiful and commands a panoramic view of the surrounding countryside.

A GROUP OF TREES is seen on the left near the summit of Silver Star. Snow-laden, their dark shapes silhouetted against the glow of the afternoon sun shining through an approaching storm.

TWO SKIERS, shown at right, enjoy Silver Star's great powder snow and beautifully groomed runs. Open daily from mid-November to early May each year for skiers, Silver Star Mountain is now open in the summer months as well. Activities at the Village include hiking and horseback riding. For the cross country enthusiast, a visit to Silver Star's new Nordic Centre is a must.

ST. ANNE'S CHURCH at the historic O'Keefe Ranch is seen on the left. This picturesque old church is one of the many original buildings that can be seen at this historic Okanagan site.

BEAUTIFUL OTTER LAKE is located on a scenic back road on our way north from O'Keefe towards Armstrong.

THE VALLEY OF SPALLUMCHEEN north of Vernon was first settled in 1866 by A.L. Fortune who wrote "And our eyes feasted on the long stretch of prairies" as he described in his journal this broad fertile north Okanagan Valley. Cattle and sheep first grazed these lush fields, later, grain replaced livestock and remains as the principle crop today.

THE TOWN OF ARMSTRONG nestles in the center of the beautiful Spallumcheen Valley. Serving a population engaged mostly in grain and dairy farming, grain elevators and feed silos are a common sight. Many fine dairy herds can be seen grazing in the lush fields. Armstrong is internationally famous for the production of "Armstrong Cheese." Every fall the town of Armstrong hosts the Interior Provincial Exhibition, an exciting annual event, which is truly a real old fashioned country "Fall Fair."

GOLDEN FIELDS OF GRAIN stretch endlessly into the far distance. Here, we see a tawny field of wheat ripe and ready for harvest. Soon, as we see on the left, a busy Okanagan farmer will be combining a bountiful crop.

A FIELD OF SWEET ALFALFA is watered one more time before it is cut and baled. The field shown on the left is near Westwold northwest of Vernon.

THE CLIFFS OF ENDERBY, shown on the right, rising majestically beyond the scenic Shuswap River.

A SPLIT RAIL FENCE, shown at upper left, guards a fertile field of riverbottom land near Enderby.

THE SHUSWAP RIVER is shown at left as it meanders through the rich and fertile riverbottom lands of the Enderby Valley. This scenic river, with it's unlimited recreational opportunities, attracts many visitors to Enderby each year.

THE CITY OF ENDERBY, located on the banks of the Shuswap River, is the head of navigation for the entire Shuswap and Thompson River system which encompass over one thousand miles of scenic waterway. An important historic center, this picturesque little town, now serves a growing number of recreational visitors as well as a local population engaged in farming and forestry.

A PICTURESQUE RED BARN is shown at left standing in the shadow of the famous cliffs of Enderby.

THE FAMOUS BRIDGE OF ENDERBY, shown on the right, as it used to be. This picturesque and much photographed old bridge across the Shuswap River at Enderby has now been replaced by a sleek modern new crossing as we can see in the picture on the left.

MARA LAKE, shown on the left, lying cool and placid beyond a glowing autumn maple. This scenic lake is part of the Shuswap-Thompson River system.

THE TOWN OF SICAMOUS, often called the "Houseboat Capital of Canada", is situated at the narrows between beautiful Mara Lake and the lovely and scenic Shuswap Lake. Focused on, and catering to visitors who have come to enjoy this beautiful waterway. Sicamous is the headquarters and home port of many of the houseboats for which this area has become famous. From Sicamous we can reach by motor boat, canoe or houseboat an entire inland waterway which includes, the Shuswap River, Mara Lake, Shuswap Lake and the Thompson River. Hundreds of miles of scenic shoreline wait to be explored. It is said that there is nothing to compare with the comfort and safety of houseboating. Indeed many families and groups of friends are getting together each year to take advantage of the unlimited recreational possibilities that can be enjoyed while houseboating.

SCENES OF SICAMOUS are seen on the right. The elevated bridge of Highway 1 crosses the Sicamous Narrows. Three locomotives pull a heavy coal train over the C.P.R. railroad bridge at the narrows. An aerial view showing some of the docks and berths of the Shuswap houseboats in the narrows. A houseboat is shown tied to the shore at a clean pebbly beach on Shuswap Lake.

SHUSWAP LAKE is seen on the left from a viewpoint on Highway 1 near the narrows at Sicamous.

THE COLDSTREAM VALLEY, at left, as seen from a viewpoint on Highway 97. Here, we have back-tracked for a moment, so that we may take a short trip up this scenic and fertile Valley.

THE TOWN OF LUMBY lies at the top of the Coldstream Valley and is the gateway to the Monashee Mountains. Although Lumby serves a diverse agricultural community, here logging and lumber is king. On the right, we can see huge stacks of fragrant, freshly sawn lumber drying in the sun beyond a scenic country stream.

LOGGING TRUCKS, like these seen on the right, heavily laden with huge loads of logs, can be seen arriving every few minutes at the several mills that are located near Lumby. Some of these logs had been harvested in logging shows which are many miles from town and were trucked a great distance to the mills located here.

A ROW OF MONSTER TIRES are seen on the right, many of these have long since been retired. These huge tires have been used on "skidders," machines that are used for skidding logs out of the bush.

A RUSTIC OLD BARN complete with broken-down fence and derelict wagon graces a farmer's field near Lumby.

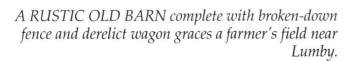

BALES OF STRAW resting in a golden field of stubble are seen on the left along Highway 6 near Cherryville. In the distance, Camel Back Mountain, a local landmark, in the Monashee foothills.

MABEL LAKE, seen on the right, is located north of Lumby on the Shuswap River system. This secluded mountain lake is becoming more popular with summer visitors, boaters and fishermen.

THE SPILLWAY AT SHUSWAP FALLS seen here in the Spring during high water. Later on, during the summer, this thundering torrent slows to a trickle, and then, dries up, as all of the waters of the Shuswap River are diverted through the turbines of the Shuswap Falls Power Station. A fish hatchery is located near Shuswap Falls and welcomes visitors throughout the summer.

BEAUTIFUL ECHO LAKE is seen on the left. This extraordinary beautiful turquoise jewel lies hidden in the narrowing top end of Creighton Valley in the foothills of the Monashee Mountains.

SUGAR LAKE, shown here on the right, is a beautifully scenic lake which is located about ten miles north of Cherryville off Highway 6. Sugar Lake forms the headwaters of the Shuswap River. Great fishing, canoeing and spectacular scenery await us here at the edge of the Monashee Mountain Range.

THE TOWN OF REVELSTOKE located on Highway 1 is the northern gateway to the Okanagan/Shuswap region. On the right, the mountains of the Big Bend Country can be seen reflecting in a backwater of the Columbia River, near the site of the Revelstoke Dam and Generating Station. A huge hydro electric project, the Revelstoke Dam is one of two dams located on the Columbia River near Revelstoke. The other is at Mica Creek approximately 150 kilometers north of Revelstoke. Between them, these two dams have an installed generating capacity that exceeds 3,500,000 kilowatts.

THE SELKIRK MOUNTAINS, shown on the left, are seen from Highway 1 near Albert Canyon and the Rogers Pass.

THE COLUMBIA RIVER BRIDGE at Revelstoke, shown on the right, provides the Columbia River crossing for Highway 1. At the western entrance of the famous Rogers Pass, Revelstoke nestles in the narrow Columbia River valley between the snow-capped peaks of the Monashee and Selkirk Mountains. Highway 1 climbs from here following the Illicillewaet River Valley towards the crest of the Rogers Pass in Glacier National Park.

THE ROGERS PASS HIGHWAY, shown here on the left, is the preferred, most direct, and scenic route east to Golden and the Canadian Rockies.

SCENIC SALMON ARM and its central pond and fountain are seen on the left overlooking Shuswap Lake.

THE TOWN OF SALMON ARM is located on Highway 1 beside the shores of beautiful Shuswap Lake. Often called "The gem of the Shuswap," Salmon Arm is the center of this year-round vacation playground.

HOUSEBOATING ON SHUSWAP LAKE is a popular summer pastime. The pictures shown on the right give us an indication why this is so. A family or a group of friends vacationing in a houseboat on Shuswap Lake need not look far before they find a beautiful sandy beach at which they can park their temporary home. Shuswap Lake is famous for its many sandy beaches. Here we see several that are located near Salmon Arm. Many houseboaters will take along or will have at their disposal a speed boat which allows them to explore the shoreline, go fishing, shopping to replenish the ship, or to enjoy water sports, such as, water skiing and tubing.

A PICTURESQUE BARN located on a farm on the outskirts of Salmon Arm is shown at left. This pastoral scene,typifies the scenic dairy and produce farms that are so much a part of this community. Green pastures, home to herds of contented Holstein cows, fields of grain, alfalfa and sweet corn can be seen from Salmon Arm's picturesque country roads.

SALMON ARM AND SHUSWAP LAKE are at the junction of Highway 1 and Highway 97. A community airport provides convenient connections between Vancouver and Calgary. C.P.R.'s Via Rail offers daily connections to Salmon Arm as part of their transcontinental service.

FISHING IN SHUSWAP LAKE is good year-round but is at its best from late Fall through to early Summer. Kamloops Trout, Lake Trout and Kokanee (landlocked salmon) are the most popular species. Each fisherman of course has his favorite rig, but generally, these fish will take lures that are readily available at local sport shops. Trolled lures such as the "Mac's Squid" and "Flatfish" are the most popular.

THE FAMOUS KAMLOOPS TROUT is the prize that most anglers pursue. Here, on the right, we see a happy lady fisherman proudly showing off two fine specimens. These two fish, weighing 18 and 15 pounds respectively, were taken in the third week of April, 1987 on a green "Mac's Squid" plug being trolled on two hundred feet of line behind an 8-oz. weight.

AN IDEAL BOAT for Shuswap Lake fishing is shown on the right. This boat is approximately 17 feet long and is powered by a powerful inboard engine. This allows the fisherman to travel quickly and safely to his favorite fishing area. Once there, he will lower the small outboard engine to provide the slower speed required for trolling. In this picture we have the opportunity also, to see one of Shuswap Lake's clean, fine sandy beaches.

A SHUSWAP LAKE MARINA is shown on the right. Facilities like this are popular with local fisherman who often leave their boat tied up at such a Marina permanently. Visiting fishermen, on the other hand, will often trailer their boats and use one of the many launching ramps that are provided. The Marina facility that we see here is located on Shuswap Lake near Little River.

103

AN OLD BARN, shown at top, is located on one of the many farms that surround Shuswap Lake. This one is near Scotch Creek.

THE SETTING SUN sinks below the dark hills beyond a Shuswap Lake pier near Sorrento.

SHUSWAP LAKE AND COPPER ISLAND are seen on the facing page. This area near Celista, is a favorite with local fishermen.

TUG BOATS ON ADAMS LAKE are used to barge equipment and to tow log booms on this large lake which is located northwest of Shuswap Lake. Adams Lake drains into Shuswap Lake via the famous Adams River.

THE ADAMS RIVER SALMON RUN is indeed an interesting natural phenomenon. Every Fall, thousands of Sockeye Salmon make their way up the Fraser-Thompson River system, returning here to the Adams River to spawn. The number of fish returning each year varies over a four-year cycle. Super runs of fish occur every four years. On the left we see several pictures of the Adams River Sockeye run of 1984.

Over the years, millions of visitors have come here to the Adams River to witness the Sockeye Salmon spawning run. Visitors are welcome to the spawning grounds, most of which are now protected by the 2400-acre Roderick Haig-Brown Conservation Area. An information center, featuring informative and colorful displays, has been established and is jointly maintained by the Fisheries Commission, The Fisheries Association of B.C. and the Department of Recreation and Conservation of British Columbia. Be sure to put on a good pair of walking boots and some warm clothing the next time you visit the Adams River. The best viewing time is during the second and third weeks of October. The main event can be viewed via a network of paths, walkways and platforms that have been provided. Pairs of the brilliantly colored Sockeye Salmon can actually be seen in the act of spawning, a truly exciting experience. As we take our leave, we resolve that on our return, we will make a day of it, bring a lunch and, oh yes, let's not forget our camera.

ADAMS LAKE shown here in the Autumn, as the morning mist begins to rise, revealing its cool placid beauty.

THE SOUTH THOMPSON VALLEY *from a point of view near Chase is seen on the left. Low storm clouds gather in the late afternoon, darkening the sky, muting the brilliant Fall colors.*

INDIAN PICTOGRAPHS *can be seen in several places in the vicinity of Chase. Seen on the left, these pictographs are located at the Niskonlith site which is high on a ridge overlooking the Thompson River. Here, two young hikers prepare to photograph these historic native graffiti.*

THE CHASE CREEK WATERFALLS, *seen on the right, are located just off Highway 1 about a mile east of the town of Chase. A few picnic tables have been provided making this a great place to pause, perhaps have a picnic lunch, or to just enjoy the scenic beauty.*

THE ADAMS RIVER BRIDGE *on the Highway to Scotch Creek, Celista and Anglemont, communities on the north shore of Shuswap Lake.*

109

THE THOMPSON RIVER is seen here on the right from a point of view just north of the new bridge at Pritchard. This newly-built crossing replaces the previous structure, an old drawbridge, which could be lifted to allow the passage of river boats. This section of the Thompson River served for many years as the main transportation link for the early settlers. Paddle Wheelers and river boats of all sizes, plied this river in great numbers to supply the gold camps of Seymour Arm , Sicamous and the upstream communities of Salmon Arm and Spallumcheen (now the city of Enderby). Today, most of the boat traffic on the Thompson River is recreational.

THE THOMPSON RIVER VALLEY between the city of Kamloops and Shuswap Lake is very scenic. The river flows gently, can be easily navigated, and provides a host of recreational possibilities. The Sternwheeler "Wanda-Sue" can be seen plying the river taking visitors on sight-seeing excursions. Water skiers and houseboaters share the river in the summer while fishermen try their luck year-round. On the left, a stately Ponderosa Pine stands guard over the placid South Thompson River near Kamloops.

THE RIVERSHORES GOLF AND COUNTRY CLUB, shown here on the right, is one of three golf courses in the Kamloops area. This beautiful course, which was designed by the renowned golf course architect Robert Trent Jones, nestles on the Valley bottom, like a huge bright green carpet, spread between the rugged sage-covered cliffs and the river shore.

THE GREAT CLAY CLIFFS OF KAMLOOPS stand along the edge of the Thompson River Valley north of Kamloops. These scenic ramparts are left over from the ice age. Composed of glacial silt, the plateau has eroded sharply at its edge, forming rows of marching cliffs, gigantic mesas and thin spires and hoodoos. On the left, the South Thompson River can be seen as it flows silently past sage-covered hills and these haunting sentinels of silt and clay.

THE HARPER RANCH lies sprawled on the west side of the South Thompson River north of Kamloops. The ranch occupies approximately 4,000 acres of lush riverbottom flatlands, sage-covered hills and rugged mountain country. Incredibly picturesque, scenes from the Harper Ranch country can be seen on the right. An old corral snuggles in the shadow of a towering cliff. Huge bales of sweet alfalfa glow in the sun waiting to feed the hungry herds this winter. A mesa, formed of silt and clay, stands alone, towering above a valley of fragrant sage. These pictures offer us only a brief glimpse of the incredible beauty of this South Thompson ranching country.
Cattle ranching began in the Kamloops area in the mid to late 1800's. The Harper Ranch, shown here, was founded in 1862 by the Harper brothers who provided beef to feed the hungry gold camps of the Caribou and Seymour Arm. In later years, the Harpers went on to establish the famous Gang Ranch in the Chilcotin country. Cattle ranching is big business around Kamloops and the high country. Some of North America's largest cattle ranches are located near here.

KAMLOOPS, THE CITY OF RAIL, is an often used phrase, that still aptly describes this interior hub city. While many centers have seen the importance of rail decline, Kamloops, has established and maintains, a position of prominence as an important center of railroading in south central British Columbia.

A MULTI-ENGINE TRAIN is seen on the right as it pauses for a moment at Kamloops Junction.

A COAL TRAIN moves slowly along the C.P.R. main line, its brightly coloured caboose following an endless line of black coal cars as they rumble on, disappearing into the distance.

THREE MIGHTY DIESEL ENGINES are seen on the left as they thunder along the Canadian Pacific main line pulling a long heavy train north of Kamloops. Scenes like this are typical, near this hub railroad city. Main lines of the C.P.R. run east and west through the city on the south side of the Thompson River. Branch rail lines run south from the city to the Okanagan Valley. On the north side of the Thompson the C.N.R. main line tracks run west and north from the City of Kamloops. Trains, railroads and railroaders have always been, and continue to be, an important part of the fabric of this city and its people. It was near this spot, on May 8th 1906, that the notorious Bill Miner and his gang of train robbers held up Canadian Pacific Imperial #97 as it pulled out of Duck Station bound for Kamloops. Miner was subsequently apprehended, tried and convicted for the robbery.

AN OLD DIESEL ENGINE, a CNR veteran of many a hard pull, waits near the shops at Kamloops Junction to be serviced and repaired.

A BEAUTIFUL FLORAL GARDEN , part of Riverside Park in Kamloops, is seen at right. This arbored entrance to a colorful commemorative display, welcomes visitors to the park.

KAMLOOPS, THE VACATION CENTER of this high country region, is noted for its dry climate. Nestled in a semi-desert glacial valley, Kamloops enjoys abundant sunshine, warm summers and mild winters. Located at the confluence of the North and South Thompson Rivers, Kamloops offers summer visitors an ideal playground. Sailing, water skiing and wind surfing are popular activities. Many species of water fowl can be seen along the Rivers. On the left, we see boaters and water skiers enjoying the river. Enthusiastic young bathers play and shout, enjoying the clear warm water and sandy shores. A group of Canada Geese watch warily from an off-shore sandbar.
The City of Kamloops is often called the Tournament Capital of British Columbia because of the many sporting events that are hosted here. Baseball, Soccer, Ice Hockey, Curling and Basketball are but a few. Horse racing and other equestrian events are held at the Kamloops Exhibition Grounds.
The Kamloops Sagebrush Theatre presents programs put on by the Kamloops Symphony Orchestra and the Western Canada Theatre Company. Elsewhere, the Kamloops Art Gallery provides a forum for local artists and touring shows.

C.N. ENGINE NO. 2141, shown on the right, is on permanent display at Riverside Park. This gigantic steam locomotive is a lasting symbol of the railroads' exciting bygone era of steam. Once, this powerful engine was a proud workhorse on the C.N. main line, operated with skill and pride by railroad engineers and firemen. Today, it stands retired, with boilers cold, at Riverside Park. It's engineers and firemen now, are delighted children at play, small hands, on a well-worn throttle, guide old Engine 2141, as it once again, chugs proudly down a make-believe track.

116

117

THE PROVINCIAL COURT HOUSE, *shown above, is located in Kamloops. Housing various government offices as well as the court rooms, major Supreme Court trials, both civil and criminal, are conducted here.*

THE B.C. LOTTERY CORPORATION *data processing headquarters is shown on the right. This impressive contemporary building, receives and tabulates lottery sales data from a network of hundreds of terminals throughout the Province.*

THE ROYAL INLAND HOSPITAL, *shown above, is a modern acute care facility. A regional referral hospital, the Royal Inland, serves the entire south central region of British Columbia.*

A REGIONAL FINANCIAL CENTER, *Kamloops is the home of many financial institutions. On the right, the regional headquarters building of the Royal Bank of Canada.*

118

KAMLOOPS, THE ECONOMIC CENTER of this south central British Columbia region, serves a diverse and upwardly mobile population. The economy of Kamloops was shaped in the past by agriculture and rail. More recently, finance, forestry and mining have grown in importance along with tourism and product distribution. Recent improvement in the overall transportation network, including the completion of the four-lane Coquihalla Highway, have made Kamloops one of the most strategic locations in the interior of British Columbia. On these pages, we see some of the modern office buildings, shopping centers and highrise apartment buildings that are located in this exciting and vibrant city.

THE FOREST INDUSTRY has in recent years moved to the forefront of the Kamloops economy. Along with mining and manufacturing, the processing of forest products has led the industrial sector here. A pulp mill, several sawmills, a plywood plant and a state-of-the-art tree nursery have located and are well established in the community.

The forest lands that surround Kamloops, as well as offering unlimited recreational opportunities, provide the raw material that sustains these Kamloops industries. The operating forest companies, along with the Ministry of Forests and Lands, are committed to managing these forest lands to provide sustained timber production as well as preserving the recreational features for enjoyment by the public.

On these pages, we see on the left, a large sawmill operation with neatly stacked lifts of freshly cut timber drying in the sun. On the right, a pulp mill and it's adjoining "hogg" farm. These facilities are operated by Weyerhaeuser Canada Limited, which is one of the major industrial companies located at Kamloops.

THE MINING INDUSTRY is important to the Kamloops economy. Several large mining companies are engaged in various mining operations near this interior city. Lornex, Highland Valley Copper and Afton Mines are working rich copper/molybdenum deposits nearby. Some of the largest open pit mining operations in Canada are carried on near Kamloops and nearby at Logan Lake.

Many of the large mining and forestry companies welcome visitors at their various operations.

123

SCENIC NICOLA LAKE, seen here on the right, is located near Meritt in the Nicola Valley. One of several lakes that can be seen on the scenic drive south from Kamloops along Highway 5.

THE EMPIRE OF GRASS, is the way that this broad expanse of ranching country in the Nicola Valley is often described. The famous Douglas Lake Ranch, located here, is one of the largest cattle ranches in Canada. Shown on the left, are several scenes typical of this vast expanse of grassland. A country road meanders through endless fields of golden bunch grass, disappearing over the horizon in the distance. A herd of plump white-faced cattle hurries home to the corrals near the main ranch buildings. Douglas Lake lies in the center of this rolling ranch country and gives it's name to the Douglas Lake Cattle Company who operate this huge ranch. The Home Ranch headquarters, located nearby, is the center of this sprawling cattle ranching operation. The Home Ranch, has a store, post office and even a small school. Visitors are welcome.

THE HISTORIC QUILCHENA HOTEL, shown on the right, stands near the junction of the Douglas Lake Road on Highway 5. This picturesque old hotel is one of the very few old style hotels that are still in operation in British Columbia. The hotel was originally built in 1908 by speculators who believed that a branch line of the C.P.R. would be built through the Nicola Valley from Meritt to Kamloops. The Railway, however, took a different route, leaving this elegant building isolated in the wilderness. Fortunately, the hotel has been preserved with it's turn-of-the-century finery virtually in tact. Fine old Victorian furniture can be seen in it's parlor, gaslights and chamber pots in the old fashioned bedrooms. You can have a drink in the Wild West Saloon, which comes complete with authentic bullet holes in the bar and billiard table. The Quilchena Hotel is truly a surviving link to the historic past of the Nicola Valley, a living legend, in this fascinating "Empire of Grass".

126

CATTLE, LOGGING AND MINING form the base of the economy of Meritt and the Nicola Valley. On the outskirts of town, we are impressed by mountainous stacks of huge logs waiting to be sawn and acres of neatly stacked lifts of newly-sawn lumber drying in the sun.

THE MINING INDUSTRY is engaged in various mining operations near this interior town. Above we see two monstrous ore carriers working at the Highland Valley Copper Mine at nearby Logan Lake.

SOME INTERESTING BUILDINGS can be seen in the Meritt-Nicola region. Shown on the facing page, top left, the picturesque old Trinity United Church at Meritt. Top right, a beautifully preserved turn-of-the-century mansion at Nicola, stands across the street from the historic Murray United Church and graveyard, also shown on the right. Center left, the newly constructed and unique church of Our Lady of Lourdes. This church, located at the junction of Highway 5 and the Douglas Lake Ranch Road, was built mostly by volunteers and native craftsmen. Bottom left, the historic Coldwater Hotel at Meritt. On the bottom right, a deserted homestead near Douglas Lake. Were there space here available, there is no doubt that many interesting stories could be told about these fine old buildings of Meritt and Nicola.

THE THOMPSON RIVER NEAR SPENCES BRIDGE, *as we can see here, is the scene of much activity during the summer months. Long trains, moving to and fro over mainline tracks on both sides of the river, are ignored, by excited groups of bathers and river rafters enjoying a picnic on the river's sandy shores.*

RIVER RAFTING *is a popular holiday activity here on the Thompson River near Spences Bridge. On the right, we see a happy group of river runners, securely clad in life jackets, setting out on an exciting river rafting adventure. The Frog, Devil's Kitchen, Witches Caldron, The Washing Machine and everyone's favorite, the Jaws of Death, are the names of but a few of the thirty or more, raft-pounding rapids, that we can shoot, on a spectacular day-long raft ride down the incredibly scenic Thompson River, as it flows south from Spences Bridge to Lytton.*

LUSH FIELDS OF SWEET ALFALFA, *like these on the right, can be seen near the twin communities of Ashcroft and Cache Creek.*

THE OLD ASHCROFT FIREHOUSE, *seen on the left, still stands and can be seen in the village of Ashcroft today.*

ASHCROFT AND CACHE CREEK *are linked historically to the famous Caribou Gold rush. "There's gold in them thar hills", is a cry that was often heard here along the Caribou Trail to the gold fields of the north. Indeed, stories still persist today of intrigue and double cross, of the legendary buried treasure, the lost cache of gold which remains undiscovered to this day.*

THE ASHCROFT MUSEUM, *shown on the left, has on display, many artifacts and relics of the great gold rush and the Caribou Trail.*

HISTORIC CACHE CREEK, *located at the junction of Highway 1 and Highway 97, is today a bustling tourist mecca. Shown on the right, this busy junction town is the gateway to the fabled Caribou and to Kamloops and the High Country.*

THE THOMPSON RIVER, shown here at right, near the historic town of Walhachin. The waters of the Thompson River from here to Spences Bridge are a favorite haunt of hearty fishermen who pursue with dedication the legendary sea-going Steelhead Trout. Many fine Steelhead are taken here each year.

THE GHOSTS OF WALHACHIN can still be seen along Highway 1 as it traverses this arid benchland along the Thompson River. A crumbling irrigation flume clings to the rocky hillside to our left. Scraggly, gnarled apple trees seem strangely out of place in this desert landscape. These curious relics are the ghostly remains of a grandiose scheme that was launched in the early 1900's by British land developers. Water was diverted from a source far to the north in Deadman Valley along miles of ditches and wooden flumes to irrigate these desert benches above the Thompson River. Fruit and apple trees were planted, crops of tobacco, corn, onions and tomatoes flourished. A townsite was built on the south bank of the Thompson River and called Walhachin (meaning abundant land in the native Indian). It is said that the grand scheme of Walhachin would have been successful had it not been for the first world war. Most of the town's young men left for the battle fields of Europe, never to return. Those remaining struggled for several years to maintain the miles of ditches and flumes which required constant repairs. Eventually, the irrigation system fell into complete disrepair and was abandoned. The sage brush, once displaced, gradually returned, until today, it again reigns supreme over this arid land. All that remains are the ghosts of Walhachin.

TWO PONDEROSA PINES, spread their gnarled branches, as they stand guard over the sun-bleached remains of Walhachin.

THE BRIDGE AT SAVONA, seen on the right, carries Highway 1 across the Thompson River just a few short yards down stream from scenic Kamloops Lake.

DEADMAN VALLEY, located a short distance off Highway 1 northwest of Savona, was the scene of some extensive and recent volcanic activity. Completely out of character but incredibly scenic, some of the curious landmarks include ,"Splitrock", a collection of beautifully colored and distorted volcanic cliffs. Huge cinder cones of volcanic ash and several unique groups of cap-stoned pinnacles.

THE HOODOOS OF DEADMAN VALLEY, shown on the left, were formed, we are told, by volcanic forces and erosion. A less plausible but more romantic explanation of their existence arises out of an obscure Indian legend. It was told that there once lived in this valley a mighty Indian chief who was slain at this very spot by five jealous companions while in the act of making love to a beautiful mountain princess. Enraged, the Great Spirit Gods of the Valley turned the five treacherous warriors into these five pillars of stone. The Great Spirit decreed, that as punishment for their murderous treachery, they must stand here on this hillside forever, to gaze upon another rock pillar, the grotesque symbol of the great slain chief's unrequieted love.

A C.N.R. FREIGHT TRAIN, is seen on the right, as it rumbles past a mainline siding at sunset, near Savona.

KAMLOOPS LAKE as seen from a point of view along Highway 1 near Savona.

A HERD OF WHITE FACED CATTLE graze on the open range south of Kamloops. Scenes like this are typical of this ranching countryside.

THE BALANCING ROCK, shown on the left, is a famous local landmark. This curious pillar, with its balanced capstone, is located near Savona overlooking Kamloops Lake.

PINANTAN LAKE, seen on the right, is one of several beautiful high country lakes located along a scenic back country road north of Kamloops. Popular with local fishermen these beautiful lakes produce firm, hard fighting, Rainbow and Kamloops trout. Hunting is good, Willow and Blue Grouse are plentiful as are White Tail and Mule deer.

THE HIGH COUNTRY surrounding Kamloops is ideally suited to ranching. Vast areas of high rolling grass lands form broad meadows like those seen on the left. Large number of white-faced cattle are raised on these ranch lands each year. Horses are still used extensively by ranch hands to herd cattle. Every fall, these colorful "cowboys" can be seen as they gather the cattle into huge herds at roundup time.

PAUL LAKE, seen here on the right, is the irrigation water reservoir for the adjoining Harper Ranch, providing irrigation water in the summer to the ranch's hay fields located in the valley bottom. This scenic lake is a favorite with campers and fishermen. Paul Lake can be reached by a good gravel road which branches off from the Yellowhead Highway near Kamloops.

142

THE HIGH LAKES like McGillivray and Morressey Lake located north of Kamloops, near Tod Mountain, are good fishing for Rainbow Trout year round.

SNOWMOBILERS AND ICE FISHERMEN, like these shown on the upper right, are frequent visitors to the high lakes during the sunny winter months.

A WARM WINTER SUNSET greets us as we drive home along the road from McGillivray Lake after a long day of snowmobiling and ice fishing.

TOD MOUNTAIN AT KAMLOOPS, like the other interior ski mountains, boasts of dry powder snow, a wide variety of different downhill runs and lots of sunshine. Tod Mountain has something for everyone. Here we see skiers enjoying both the groomed and powder runs.

THE TOP OF THE WORLD SUMMIT, shown here, is where the many ski runs begin. Choose a smoothly groomed or untracked powder run, either way you are in for an exhilarating treat.

A WORLD OF CONTRAST, is this alpine land near the summit of Tod Mountain. On the right, we see two scenes, one of a frozen winter wonderland, the other, of a lush green alpine meadow. The two beautiful extremes of Tod Mountain.

146

A HIGH MEADOW above the timberline near the summit of Tod Mountain, is seen on the right, ablaze with summer wild flowers. While alpine skiers rarely visit their favourite mountain during the summer, thereby missing a colourful and spectacular scenic event, hikers and mountaineers, on the other hand, have known about, and enjoyed these alpine meadows for many years. Recently, ski mountains such as Tod, Silver Star and Big White, have begun to offer summertime uphill transportation by chairlift, thereby giving many more people the opportunity to enjoy the annual display of wildflowers. The best time to catch the peak of the wild flowers are the clear warm days of early August.

ALPINE WILD FLOWERS bloom in profusion on the high mountain meadows of the Okanagan and High Country each summer. Dozens of species can be observed. Some of the more common varieties are shown here. Top left, the Purple Lupine is very common as is the brilliant Fireweed shown on the top right. The Indian Paintbrush shown at left is a brilliant and colorful native of the alpine meadowlands as is the colorful Columbine seen here, below left. Hikers need not trek to the top of mountains to enjoy displays of wild flowers. In the Spring the hills and meadows of the Okanagan and High Country are covered with many kinds of wild flowers. Fields of Balsam-Root Sunflowers can be seen in the early Spring along the sage covered hills surrounding the lower lakes. Daisies and Dandelions grow in profusion along the country roadsides, as does the Fireweed and Lupine. For a special treat though, it is hard to match the thrill and exhilaration of a summit alpine hike to catch the wild flowers of summer.

A DISPLAY OF FIREWEED is seen on the facing page. A carpet of brilliant Fireweed spills over and covers the summer ski run at Mt. Tod.